45 Chair Exercises For Seniors

Best Chair Exercises for Improved Mobility, Joint Health, Balance, Pain Relief, and Injury Prevention

Owen Brown

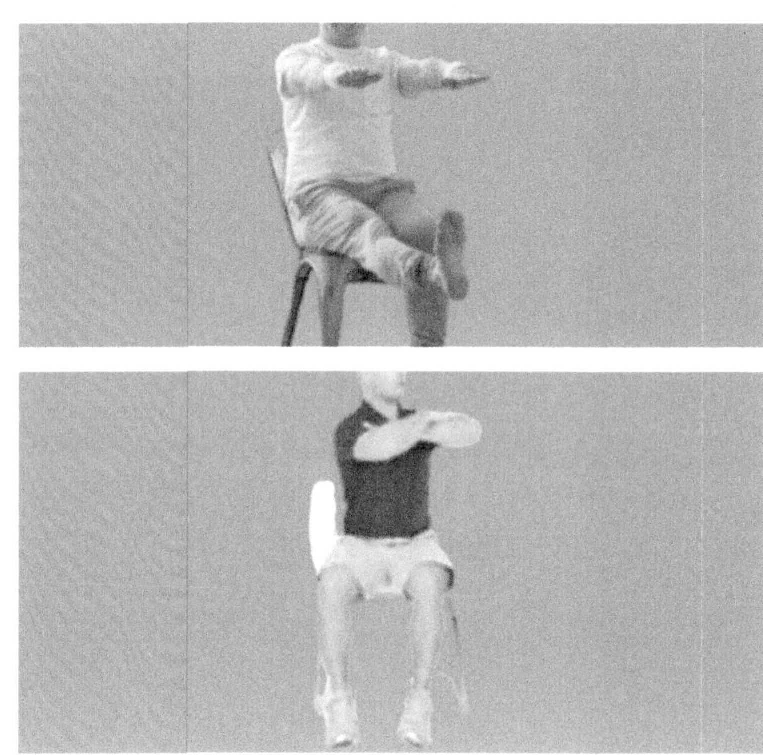

Table of Contents

Flexibility Exercises in a Sitting Position.

Seated Chest Exercises

Introduction

The secret to a healthier lifestyle as an older adult is physical fitness, but many seniors do not get the exercise they require. Only 15% of people aged 65 to 74 say they are physically active regularly. Regular workouts can help you maintain your independence as you get older. If you have a long-term medical condition like diabetes or heart disease, keeping fit can be beneficial. In addition, studies show that regular physical activity can elevate your mood.

When seniors lose their physical fitness, it can be difficult to regain it. Two weeks of sedentary lifestyle can have a detrimental effect on older adults' blood sugar and muscular condition, and the losses are not recouped with two weeks of normal movement.

If these exercises cause any discomfort, the patient should stop and consult with a medical professional.

Part 1

Why Chair Exercise

For older adults who are concerned about over-exercising or falling during the workout, chair exercises may be the solution.

When it comes to exercising, most people are instructed to complete a specific number of reps and sets. Seniors, particularly those who are just starting an exercise session, should pay closer attention to the quality of their moves. If you find yourself unable to maintain proper posture and proper form, stop the activity. The longer you continue to exercise with bad form, the greater the chance of injury.

Getting Started

Are you ready to begin your seated exercise program? A chair and a positive attitude are all you need! Getting started is simple, and there are numerous several exercises to choose from.

Ideal Chair

Choose a comfortable chair. The most comfortable chair will have a straight back as well as be stable. Please do not include any kind of wheel. There is no need to bring rolling chairs into the workout space. You'll need a chair with a soft cushion, but not one that's so deep that you'll fall asleep. A sturdily constructed kitchen chair is an excellent choice.

Part 2

When Should A Seniors Consider Chair Exercise?

Aging can make it more difficult to exercise and put more stress on your joints and muscles. Pain and injury can result from an increase in tension. To avoid the pain and injury that can be caused by overly intense exercise, it is critical to maintain a healthy weight and exercise regimen. Chair exercises for seniors are the ideal solution for anyone over the age of 60 who is struggling with this issue. Maintaining a healthy lifestyle is easier with their assistance.

You may be a good candidate for chair exercises if you fit any of the following descriptions:

Balance issues and an increased risk of falling while exercising

Stiffness in the joints that makes it difficult to stand

The inability to move one's body freely

Recuperating from an injury or a surgical procedure

If you're just starting a workout regimen, take it easy at first and work your way up to standing exercises.

Want a change of pace in your fitness regimen?

Part 3

Benefits of Chair Exercises for Seniors

A seated workout provides all of the advantages of a standing workout without the risk. Improved mobility and variety of motion can be achieved through chair exercises. As a result of the increased muscle strength and stability, falls and injuries can be avoided. Regular chair exercise will result in an improvement in your overall wellbeing and fitness after a few weeks of consistent engagement. In addition, you'll have a more enjoyable day and your everyday life will be less stressful.

Chair exercises for the elderly have several advantages, including:

The ability to move more freely and with more flexibility

Reduced pain and stiffness in the joints

Strengthened muscles and better balance

Blood flow is improved.

Improved mood and focus

Reduced levels of stress

Get a seat and start working out!

What Do I Need

If you're an elderly person, chair exercises might be your best bet. As a result, they allow seniors who would otherwise be unable to exercise regularly to improve their strength, cardiovascular fitness, and mobility without the risk of injury associated with traditional exercise routines. There are fewer risks of aggravating joint pain when exercising while seated. Chair exercises can help those recovering from surgery or an injury in the same way that standing routines do. You don't need anything more than a sturdy chair and a strong desire to improve your health and strength to get started.

Part 4

Stretching

Stretching is a critical component of a healthy lifestyle. Keeping the body flexible and relaxed after workouts have numerous benefits, and no fitness professional or physical therapist would disagree. It's a no-brainer in the fitness world.

Flexibility exercises can be done while either standing or laying down on the floor.

How Often Should a Senior Stretch?

The number of times a person should stretch each week after the age of 65 will vary based on their level of tension and mobility requirements.

Stretching doesn't have to be limited to specific times of the day, but rather to the number of times a day that you stretch. To get the most out of the stretches, set aside 10-15 minutes a day. It is important to take deep breaths while stretching to help calm the body and mind.

When To Stretch

Stretching is an issue that has sparked much debate. Doctors and fitness experts disagree on the best times of day and times of day to do stretches.

It's better to stretch frequently rather than for a long time because the frequency trains the tissue more effectively. For a senior, longer sessions may be too much at once or risk overworking the muscles.

Part 5

Chair Exercises for Seniors

A seated exercise is a lot more than just moving your body. With chair workouts, you can improve your cardiovascular health as well as your muscular power and flexibility. The following are the best chair workouts for older adults. Incorporate one or two workouts from each category into your chair fitness regime to ensure a balanced exercise.

Warm-Up

Easy Chair Exercises to Get You Warmed Up

A warm-up is a necessary first step in any exercise regimen. Preparing the muscles by relaxing and warming them significantly reduces the risk of injury. These seated workouts for the elderly will help you get warmed up.

Neck Stretch

Till you get a good stretch, sit up straight and gradually tilt your head to the right shoulder. As you maintain this position, slowly lower your left arm to the ground and the side.

The left side of your neck should feel stretched after doing this. Let go, and then switch sides.

Repeat on the opposite side for 2 to 5 reps.

These stretches will get your neck and upper back muscles warmed up so you can do arm workouts afterward.

Shoulder Circles

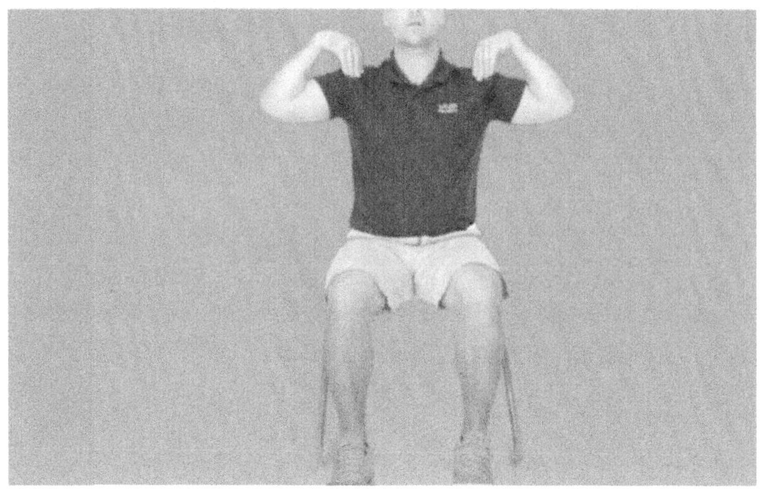

Place your fingers on your shoulders in a sitting position and relax.

Do twelve reps of the shoulder circle. Perform twelve reps of the exercise in the opposite direction.

This workout warms up shoulder muscles and reduces tension.

Seated-Backbend

Sets: 2-3

Reps: 8-12

Take a seat on the chair's edge and relax comfortably. Maintain a straight spine and upright back to protect the core. Keep your feet on the ground at all times. Be sure to keep your hips and lower body firmly in place at all times.

Put your hands on your hips.

Let the stomach push out as you slowly arch your back, then lean back using only your upper body.

Stretch the back in this position until you feel a good stretch.

Set a timer for about 10-20 seconds, then slowly come back to where you were before.

The number of times you repeat the pattern is up to you.

Seated-Overhead-Stretch

Take a seat on the chair's edge and relax comfortably. Maintain a straight spine and upright back to protect the core.

Keep your feet on the ground at all times. Be sure to keep your hips and lower body firmly in place at all times.

Put your hands on your hips.

Hands should be slowly raised overhead, interlocking at the top.

Stretching the abdomen can be achieved by arching one's back inward and pushing one's stomach out.

Then, return to the starting position after a ten-to-twenty-second hold.

Repeat 3-5 times, or as many times as necessary to achieve relaxation.

Seated-Hip-Stretch

Sets: 2-3

Reps: 10

The hips play a major role in our daily routines. If a senior is hunching over, having difficulty moving their hips, or experiencing pain in the general area of their hips, this stretch may be beneficial.

The chair is ready for you to take a seat. Maintain a straight spine and upright back to protect the core. Keep your feet on the ground at all times.

Create a triangle between the legs by crossing one leg over the other. Assuring that the ankle of the crossed leg extends beyond that of the other.

Maintaining a straight spine and a tight core, slowly bend the upper body forward. When you feel resistance in either your glutes or your hips, you should stop.

Afterward, switch sides and repeat the process for another 10-20 seconds.

Repeat 3-5 times per leg, or as much as you feel comfortable.

Chair Exercises for Arms

Increased muscle mass can improve one's balance and stability, reducing the chances of tripping and falling. Having more strength makes life, in general, a lot simpler. Life is more enjoyable when getting around isn't a hassle. Lifting heavy luggage and other objects may reinforce the idea of your better health and fitness.

Bicep Curls

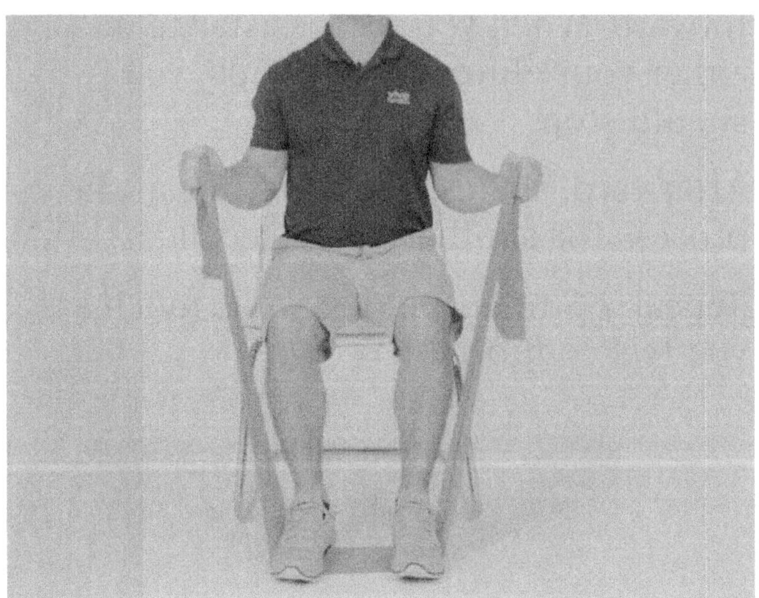

Bicep curls can be done anywhere with the simple use of resistance bands.

First, choose an X-level resistance band (from light to heavy), and then place your feet shoulder-width apart on the resistance band.

As you grip the handles of your bands, with your palms facing upward, raise your hands to your shoulders.

Gradually lower the bands while keeping your elbows at your sides.

Do this for a total of four sets of ten repetitions. Dumbbells, especially small ones, will work well.

Seated Row

Keep your knees bent and your feet firmly planted on the floor. Keeping your arms out in front of you, keep them bent a little, with your thumbs pointing upward.

Raise your elbows so that they are in line with your body, and then squeeze your shoulder blades together as you do so.

Repeat this motion 8 to 10 times. Wearing wrist weights can increase the difficulty of the exercise.

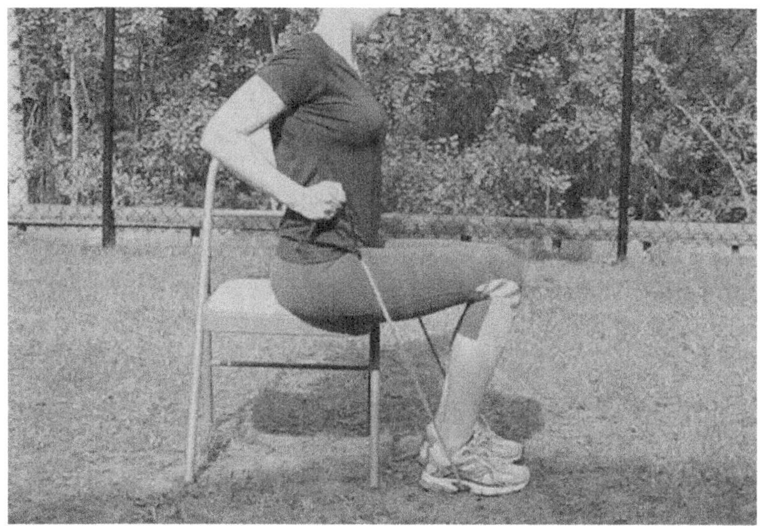

This exercise will improve your shoulders, chest, and upper back while putting minimal pressure on your joints.

Shoulder Rolls

With your feet firmly planted on the floor, sit up tall. Slightly raise your shoulders closer to your ears and gradually rotate them in a circle—backward, downward, forward, and then back upwards again.

Reverse the movement when you've reached the top.

It's important to roll your shoulders in all directions. 10 reps each way, total 20. This exercise will help you build the muscles you need for lifting heavy items.

Seated-Shoulder-Press

Sets: 2-3

Reps: 8-12

Strength, mobility, and endurance will all improve as a result of the seated shoulder press.

Dumbbells or a resistance band can be used in place of a seat, or you can simply sit on it and keep it at the same length on both sides of your body.

Sit with your hips as far back as possible in a comfortable chair.

Make sure that the back of the chair is firmly attached to the backrest of the couch.

Keep your core (abs and lumbar) in good shape.

The best place to start is with both elbows spread out to the sides of the body and under the shoulders.

The chest should be pushed outward.

Holding the dumbbells with palms facing forward, maintain a straight posture.

The arms should be fully extended, reaching above the head, at this point (or get to a range that feels most comfortable). Keep your hands apart and your arms parallel to the ground.

Slowly return the hands to the starting position while keeping the elbows spread after reaching the maximum extent of arm extension. Rather than keeping the elbows tucked in, keep them extended until you feel a slight pinch (not pain) between your shoulder blades.

Seated-Front-Shoulder-Raises

Sets: 2-3

Reps: 8-12

This is a great way to practice extending your arm forward while holding an object in front of your body.

Grab a pair of dumbbells, a resistance band, or a medicine ball and start working out.

Sit with your hips as far back as possible in a comfortable chair.

Make sure that the back of the chair is firmly attached to the backrest of the couch.

Keep your core (abs and lumbar) in good shape. The chest should be pushed outward.

When working with dumbbells, keep your arms at your sides and hang naturally with your palms facing inward.

It's best to use an elastic band for this exercise, but you can also sit on the band and slide it under the seat. Then, with your hands by your sides, let them hang naturally, palms facing in toward your midsection.

Keep your hands on either side of the ball while holding a medicine ball at your lap's edge for stability.

Continue to raise the arms in front of the body while keeping the palms facing forward.

When the hands are directly in front of your eyes and your arms are parallel to the floor, come to a complete halt.

Retrace your steps back to the starting point.

Chair Workouts for Legs

Even though strengthening your legs while seated may seem unattainable, it is not. The quads, lower body, and calves will all benefit from the chair leg workout listed below.

Tip Toeing

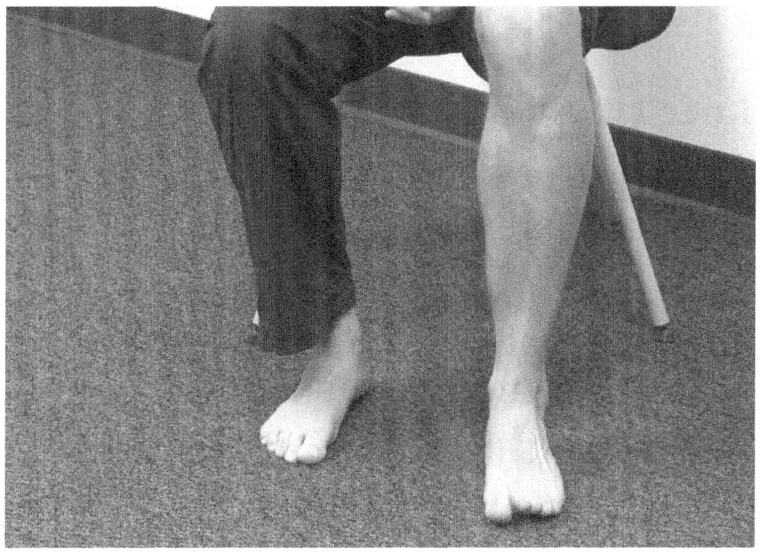

Straighten your back and fix your feet firmly on the floor. You can do this by bending your toes inward and then outward.

Keeping your legs straight while sitting at the end of your chair will increase the intensity of this workout even further.

Keep your heels firmly planted as you raise your toes and then lower them. Using this modification, the range of motion can be increased. Strengthen your calf and shin muscles with 8 to 10 repetitions of this exercise. It's these muscles that help you climb the stairs and carry out your daily routine.

Knee Lifts

Put your feet firmly on the floor with your back straight.

Take a few deep breaths and slowly bring your right knee up toward your chest before bringing it back down.

Do this on the other side. Do 10 reps on each leg for a total of 30.

Pause for a 5 at the top of the moves for an extra challenge.

The quadriceps are the biggest muscle group, and this exercise helps to strengthen them.

Strengthening your quadriceps will make you grow stronger and capable in every aspect of your life.

As your strength increases, you might want to add ankle weights to your routine for a little extra challenge.

Sit-to-Stands

Sets: 2-3

Reps: 8-12

Close your eyes and lean back in your chair.

Stay in good shape with your core. The chest should be pushed outward.

Your feet should be facing forward or slightly outward on both sides, and your hands should be in a position where they are convenient for maintaining balance.

Slowly raise yourself from the chair until you can stand unassisted.

As you get up from a seated to a standing position, keep your body in a straight line from your midsection to the outside edges of your knees. The hips, not the knees, are the only way to rise from the floor during this exercise.

Return to the starting position of your chair while checking the placement of your knees.

It's always a good idea to keep your glutes (buttocks) squeezed together as you rise from a sitting to a standing position.

Modified Squats

Sets: 2-3

Reps: 8-12

Place the seat in front of your body so that the back of the seat faces you. Retract your feet just a little bit from the chair.

Aim to keep your weight in line with the midpoint of the chair. Put your hands together in a fist in front of you.

Aim for a hip-width distance between your feet, with both of them directly under your body.

Toes should point forward or away from the body.

As you lower your buttocks toward the floor, keep your knees bent behind your toes and loosen your hips. Push both knees out and away from your body to prevent them from collapsing.

When you've reached a complete halt in your squat, push yourself back up to a standing posture.

For added stability, lean the chair's front end against a wall. Alternatively, if the chair's back is particularly high, you can place your hands directly on top of it to provide additional support.

Knee Extension

Sets: 2-3

Reps: 10

Sit back in a comfortable chair with your hips as far back as you can. Ensure that the seat's back is securely attached to the couch's backrest.

Keep your core in good shape. The chest should be pushed outward.

Make sure you keep your feet firmly on the ground by putting your hands on the sides of the chair.

A 90 ° angle should be maintained with the chair and both legs.

In front of you, raise one leg to its highest point in the air. Return the other leg to its original position to maintain balance.

Lie on your back with one leg bent at a 90-degree angle.

To count as a single set of exercises, do the same thing for both legs.

Heel Slides

Sets: 2-3

Reps: 15

Due to the strain on the joints, this exercise may not be suitable for seniors with knee pain. Elderly people with knee pain should avoid activities that place excessive strain on their joints. To avoid scuff marks on the floor, place a towel or blanket in front of the seat.

Close your eyes and lean back in your chair.

Keep your core in good shape. The chest should be pushed outward.

Make sure you keep your feet firmly on the ground by putting your hands on the sides of the seat.

Position one leg out in front of the body, with the toes pointing forward. Extended legs should have their feet diagonally aligned with the hips. If you're using blankets or other items, place your foot on top of those. You should keep your other leg straight, with your foot firmly planted on the ground, and your knee slightly bent.

To get the other leg to bend at the knee, you need to keep the foot flat on the floor and slowly drag it toward your body. Keep your other leg bent.

Keep the leg extended while maintaining the pressure.

A single repetition occurs when the foot is pulled back to the starting position and then pushed back to the starting position.

Calf Raises

Sets: 2-3

Reps: 8-12

Calf raises can help stretch tight muscles and joints in the lower leg for seniors who have trouble squatting due to tight calves.

In a comfortable chair, place your hips back as far as possible. Ensure that the seat's back is securely attached to the couch's backrest.

Keep your core in good shape. The chest should be pushed outward.

Make sure you keep your feet firmly on the ground by putting your hands on the sides of the chair.

A 90-degree angle should be maintained with the chair and both legs. Keep your feet on a flat surface at all times.

Slowly, raise the heels of your feet above the ground while keeping your toes strongly fixed on the ground.

Step back with both feet in the starting position.

For a "burning" sensation in the calves, perform at least 20 repetitions of this exercise.

This movement can be made more difficult by placing a medical ball or other weight of equal value near the edge of the lap (almost to the knees). To ensure that both feet have the full range of motion, you can place a shallow object (about 3-4 inches off the ground) under both of them.

Chair Exercise For Your Core

Improving your sense of balance and steadiness begins with a well-developed core and abdominal muscles. Perform these chair core strengthening exercises for seniors to strengthen your muscles and prevent falls. Chair workouts are excellent for toning the lower back, abs, and glutes. The following are exercises to build a strong core

Tummy Twists for Abdominals

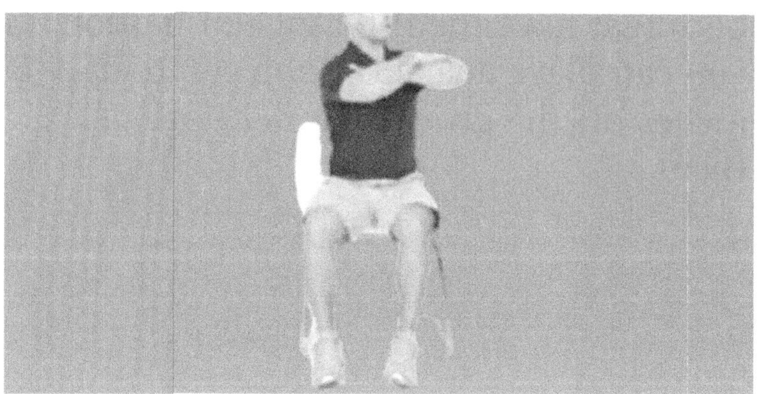

Straighten your back and fix your legs firmly on the floor.

Your elbows should be at your sides, and your forearms should be extended out in front of you so that your arms form a 90-degree angle.

Lie on your back with your upper torso facing the left. Imagine you're squeezing your tummy toward your spine, maintaining your lower body in a neutral position.

To make a right turn, go back to the center.

Do a total of 15 reps, ten on each side.

Maintaining good posture is made easier by working your obliques (a group of abdominal muscles involved in rotating your trunk). Improve your posture with one of the best back braces.

Captain's Chair

It's important to get a sturdy chair. Straighten your back and hold on to the seat's edges. Lift your feet off the ground one at a time.

Move your knees toward your torso. Slowly bring your feet back to the floor while squeezing your abs.

Don't push yourself past where you're at right now. When it comes to exercising, it doesn't matter how high you can raise your feet.

Abdominals, glutes, and other core muscles will all benefit from this workout.

Knees-to-Chest Pose

Sets: 2-3

Reps: 8-12

It's okay to lean back in your chair without feeling like you're going to collapse.

Maintain a straight spine and a tight core (abdominals and lumbar). The chest should be pushed outward.

Make sure you keep your feet firmly on the ground by putting your hands on the sides of the chair.

Stand with your feet shoulder-width apart and your toes pointed up toward the sky ceiling. The hips should be aligned with the center of the feet, and the feet should be parallel to the others.

Slowly bring your legs closer to your body while keeping your knees bent. During this exercise, your knees must remain as close to your chest as possible.

Then slowly and deliberately go back to the beginning position and do it all over once more. This is one representative.

Also, you can do this exercise with just one leg. Before you begin lifting, make sure your opposite leg is firmly planted on the ground.

Leg Raises Extensions

When you lean back in your chair, you don't have to worry about falling over.

Straighten your spine while keeping your core engaged (abdominals and lumbar). When performing this move, make sure your chest is protruding as far out as possible.

Put your hands on the chair's sides to keep your feet firmly on the ground.

Place your feet wide apart and point your toes toward the ceiling. To keep your hips in line with your feet, your feet should be positioned diagonally.

When attempting to raise one leg, it's important to keep your body's still and lift it as high as you can without moving the leg. At this point, there is no need to move your other leg.

Step backward and forwards while gently lowering one leg back to the initial position.

Repeat, 2 rep.

It's important to keep in mind that this exercise can be performed solely with one leg. Before beginning to lift the leg, make sure the opposite leg is firmly planted on the ground.

Leg Kicks

Sets: 2-3

Reps: 15

It's okay to tilt back in your chair without feeling like you're going to fall.

Maintain a straight spine and a tight core (abdominals and lumbar).

Make sure you keep your feet firmly on the ground by putting your hands on the sides of the chair.

Place your feet wide apart in front of your body and point your toes in the direction you want to go.

The hips should be aligned with the center of the feet, and the feet should be parallel to each other.

It's important to stabilize yourself by slowly leaning your upper body back when you shift your weight forward with both feet.

Without moving the center of your body, lift one leg to the highest point possible (hopefully parallel to your hips).

Step back and slowly lower the leg until it reaches its starting position, then repeat with the other leg.

Imagining a person swimming and kicking their legs in the water is an excellent metaphor for this movement.

Imagining a person swimming and kicking their legs in the water is an excellent metaphor for this movement.

Keep your feet off the ground as much as possible during this exercise so that it becomes more difficult. You can practice this movement by focusing on just one leg at a time. Lifting should only begin when the other feet are firmly on the ground.

Modified Planks

Stand with your back to the chair so that you're facing it straight ahead with your body.

Place your hands on either side of the chair's backrest, palms facing each other.

Shift your feet backward a few feet until your body is in a diagonal position in front of the chair while keeping both arms slightly bent at the elbows.

It is important to keep the buttocks firmly planted on the ground and to avoid arching one's back.

A straight line should run down the middle of the body, from the shoulders to the heels. If a senior feels resistance (tension) in their core, they're in the right place to begin.

Take a short break by standing or sitting up after 30 seconds (or however long you feel comfortable doing so without experiencing any pain).

Repeat a total of three to four times.

For added stability, lean the chair against a wall.

Chair Aerobics for Cardio

Heart attacks can be prevented and your quality of life enhanced if you improve your heart health. One of the best ways to ease the burden of daily life for the elderly is to engage in chair workouts. Is climbing the stairs making you exhausted? Chair exercises will improve your cardiovascular and respiratory health, preparing you to take on the world.

Jumping Jacks in a chair

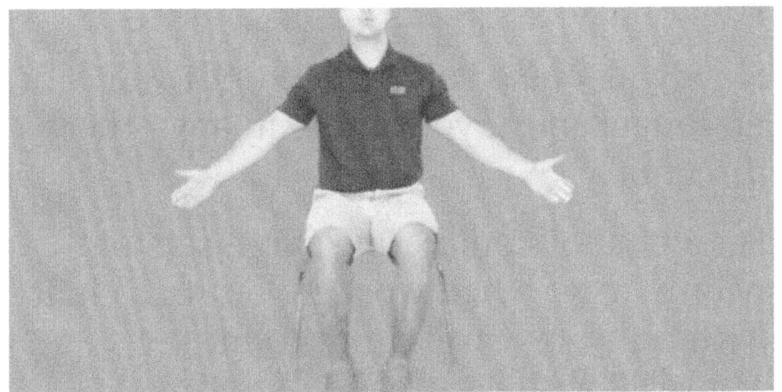

Keep your back straight and your seat firmly riveted. As you would with a standard jumping jack, extend your arms out to the sides and then up above your head.

Before re-raising them, lower them to your sides.

Slowly increase your speed until you can no longer move your arms in any other direction.

Set a goal of completing three sets of twenty reps. when working out in a chair with arms, be careful not to hit the armrests with your hands or arms.

Skater Switch

While seated on the edge of a chair, knees slightly bent and place your toe on the ground with your right foot.

Make a straight outward arc with your left leg, pointing your toes in the air. Stretch forward while extending your arms straight ahead of you.

To perform this exercise correctly, you will need to bend at the waist and reach with your left arm to your right foot's sole.

Straighten your back and bring your arms back in front of you. After 10 repetitions of this activity, swap your legs and repeat the moves for another 10 repetitions.

Interchange left and right leg positions rapidly between reps to make this exercise even more challenging.

Running a chair

As you sit, extend your legs straight out in front of you with your toes pointed forward and your arms bent at the elbows.

Your shoulders should barely touch the back of your chair when you lean back slightly in your chair.

Raise your feet slowly off the ground. Perform a running motion by bending one knee while the other is extended and then switching.

Hold on to the armrests or seat edges for support if required.

Seated Pedaling

A pedal workout is required for this moderate cardiovascular exercise, but it's worth it.

Sit on a sturdy chair or couch that won't tip over.

Depending on your strength and ability, you can choose between mild/moderate levels of tension. For approximately 25 to 30 minutes, simply put your feet on the pedals and pedal. The rubber feet keep it in place while you exercise, allowing you to read or watch TV at the same time.

Seated Tap Dance

Be sure to keep your feet gently planted on the ground and your knees slightly bent while you're sitting.

Gently tap the heel of one of your feet on the ground while extending your other leg out.

Point your toes and tap them on the floor while keeping your leg extended. Return to the heel-tapping position and flex your foot.

Repeat with the other leg. 3 to 5 mins of "tap dancing" are recommended.

Set an alarm and strive to workouts for a little extended period each time.

Flexibility Exercises in a Sitting Position.

Everything, from tying your shoe to reaching for the top shelf, is more enjoyable when you have a full range of motion. Allowing you to carry out your daily routines is made easier by a healthy level of flexibility. After you've completed your workout, perform these exercises to help loosen up your muscles.

Seated Forward Bend

Performing these moves will help to stretch your lower and upper back.

Position your feet firmly on the ground as you widen your stance.

Lie down on your back with your torso tucked in between your knees.

Loosen up your neck and bring your hands to your feet to create a meditative state. As soon as you feel a stretch, stay in the stretched position for thirty seconds before slowly returning to your previous position.

Then do it three times.

Knee to Chest

Keep your left foot firmly planted on the ground and your back straight.

Take hold of the back of your right knee and gradually bring it toward your chest till you experience a stretch.

Do this with your left leg after 30 seconds of holding the position. Execute three repetitions of each side.

To avoid injury, it is important to have flexible hamstrings and glutes, which this exercise targets.

Ankle Rotations

Straighten your back and place your other ankle on the knee of the opposite leg.

Make a circle with your ankle. Do 10 clockwise and 10 counterclockwise rotations.

Stretch your toes even further by pointing them inward.

Sit and Reach

Kneel on the floor with your back straight. You can do this by extending your upper body straight up toward the sky.

Feel the stretch in your torso as you lift your body upward. Stretch your neck and shoulders by focusing your gaze on your hand.

To change sides, hold the position for 5 - 10 secs, and then change back. Work your way around the room 3 times in total.

Seated Chest Exercises

Chest Press While Sitting

Sets: 2-3

Reps: 8-10

A compound movement uses multiple muscles at once, such as the chest, shoulders, and triceps in this case.

Grab a band of resistance.

Make sure the resistance band is positioned directly behind your back, just under your shoulders. Make sure the resistance band cannot move on the back of the chair; moving it during the exercise can cause injury or target the wrong muscle groups. As an alternative, have a senior's family member help install some shelving brackets on the back of the chair to keep the band in the proper location.

Sit with your hips as far back as possible in a comfortable chair.

Make sure that the back of the chair is firmly attached to the backrest of the couch.

Keep your core (abs and lumbar) in good shape. The chest should be pushed outward.

Keep your elbows bent and parallel to your shoulders, with your palms facing down. Shoulder-width apart, the hands must be placed just outside of each other.

The arms should not be touching each other when pushing the resistance band forward.

Slowly return to where you started

Please note: If you don't have enough tension in your resistance band, you can wrap it around another stable object like a post or beam.

Push-Ups (Modified)

Sets: 2-3

Reps: 8-12

Stand while facing the chair.

Place your hands on either side of the chair's backrest, palms facing each other.

Shift your feet backward a few feet until your body is in a diagonal position in front of the chair while keeping both arms slightly bent at the elbows. It is important to keep the buttocks firmly planted on the ground and to avoid arching one's back.

A straight line should run down the middle of the body, from the shoulders to the heels. If a senior feels resistance (tension) in their core, they're in the right place to begin.

to maintain good posture, keep your elbows close to your sides.

Elbows slowly bend inward, bringing your body closer to the seat.

Push back to the starting position as soon as the chin touches the chair (or as close to the chair as possible).

For added stability, lean the chair against a wall. If the chair isn't against a wall, make sure it won't slosh around while you're working out. Sweaty palms could cause the chair to slip from your grasp.

Triceps

Sets: 2-3

Reps: 6-10

You'll need a dumbbell to do this.

Sit with your hips as far back as possible in a comfortable chair. Make sure that the back of the chair is firmly attached to the backrest of the couch.

Keep your core (abs and lumbar) in good shape. The chest should be pushed outward.

Maintain a "V" shape with your hands behind your head and both elbows raised above your head. Assist the elbow by using the other hand to hold it in place. In this position, keep the assisting hand (without applying too much pressure). The palm holding the dumbbell should be facing the user's head.

Lift the dumbbell-laden arm over your head until it reaches its full extension.

To return to your starting position, slowly lower your forearm.

Continue with the other arm.